SEMELE

An Opera *by*

WILLIAM CONGREVE

with the alterations

adopted by

HANDEL

As performed at the
NEW THEATRE, CAMBRIDGE
10–14 *February* 1925

CAMBRIDGE
AT THE UNIVERSITY PRESS
1925

CAMBRIDGE UNIVERSITY PRESS
Cambridge, New York, Melbourne, Madrid, Cape Town,
Singapore, São Paulo, Delhi, Mexico City

Cambridge University Press
The Edinburgh Building, Cambridge CB2 8RU, UK

Published in the United States of America by Cambridge University Press, New York

www.cambridge.org
Information on this title: www.cambridge.org/9781107675766

First published 1925
Re-issued 2013

A catalogue record for this publication is available from the British Library

ISBN 978-1-107-67576-6 Paperback

EDITOR'S NOTE

THE following text has been compiled from the 1710 edition of Congreve's works and the altered version adopted by Handel and published in 1762.

All the lines omitted by the composer are here printed in smaller type, and his interpolations are set within square brackets. No account has been taken of slight differences in the texts.

In rearranging the work for the stage it has been necessary to make certain transpositions and omissions : these are noted as they occur.

D. D. A.

ARGUMENT

Introductory to the

OPERA of *SEMELE.*

Fter Jupiter's *Amour with* Europa, *the Daughter of* Agenor, *King of* Phænicia, *he again incenses* Juno *by a new Affair in the same Family;* viz. *with* Semele, *Niece to* Europa, *and Daughter to* Cadmus *King of* Thebes. Semele *is on the Point of Marriage with* Athamas; *which Marriage is about to be solemniz'd in the Temple of* Juno, *Goddess of Marriages, when* Jupiter *by ill Omens interrupts the Ceremony; and afterward transports* Semele *to a private Abode prepar'd for her.* Juno, *after many Contrivances, at length assumes the Shape and Voice of* Ino, *Sister to* Semele; *by the help of which Disguise, and artful Insinuations, she prevails with her to make a Request to* Jupiter, *which being granted must end in her utter Ruin.*

This Fable is related in Ovid. Metam. L. 3. *but, there,* Juno *is said to impose on* Semele *in the Shape of an old* Woman, *her Nurse.* 'Tis hoped, *the Liberty taken in substituting* Ino *instead of the old* Woman *will be excus'd: It was done, because* Ino *is interwoven in the Design by her Love of*

Athamas; *to whom ſhe was marry'd, according to*
Ovid; *and, becauſe her Character bears a Pro-*
portion with the Dignity of the other Perſons re-
preſented. This Reaſon, it is preſumed, may be
allowed in a Thing intirely fictitious; and more
eſpecially being repreſented under the Title of an
Opera, *where greater Abſurdities are every Day*
excus'd.

It was not thought requiſite to have any Regard
either to Rhyme, or Equality of Meaſure, in the
Lines of that Part of the Dialogue which was
deſign'd for the Recitative Stile *in Muſick. For*
as that Stile in Muſick is not confin'd to the ſtrict
Obſervation of Time *and* Meaſure, *which is re-*
quir'd in the Compoſition of Airs *and* Sonata's, *ſo*
neither is it neceſſary that the ſame Exactneſs in
Numbers, Rhymes, or Meaſure, ſhould be obſerved
in Words deſign'd to be ſet in that manner, which
muſt ever be obſerved in the Formation of Odes *and*
Sonnets. *For, what they call* Recitative *in Muſick,*
is only a more tuneable Speaking; it is a kind of
Proſe in Muſick; its Beauty conſiſts in coming near
Nature, and in improving the natural Accents of
Words by more Pathetick or Emphatical Tones.

Perſons Repreſented.

Jupiter.
Cadmus, King of *Thebes.*
Athamas, A Prince of *Bœotia,* in Love with and design'd to marry *Semele.*
Somnus.
Apollo.
Cupid.
Zephyrs.
Loves.
Shepherds.
Satyrs.
Juno.
Iris.
Semele, Daughter to *Cadmus,* beloved by and in Love with *Jupiter.*
Ino, Siſter to *Semele,* in Love with *Athamas.*
Shepherdeſſes.
Chief Prieſt of *Juno,* other Prieſts and Augurs.

[*Chorus of* Prieſts *and* Augurs.
 Chorus of Loves *and* Zephyrs.
 Chorus of Nymphs *and* Swains.
 Attendants.]

SCENE *BŒOTIA.*

[*N.B.* The Lines marked thus " are omitted in the Representation on account of the Length of the Piece.]

S E M E L E.

ACT I. SCENE I.

The SCENE *is the Temple of* Juno, *near the Altar is a Golden Image of the Goddefs. Priefts are in their Solemnities, as after a Sacrifice newly offer'd; Flames arife from the Altar, and the Statue of* Juno *is feen to bow.*

CADMUS, ATHAMAS, SEMELE, *and* I N O. [*and Chorus of* Priefts.]

FIRST PRIEST.

[Recitative *accompany'd.*]

Ehold aufpicious Flafhes rife; *Juno* accepts our Sacrifice; The grateful Odour fwift afcends, And fee the Golden Image bends.

FIRST and SECOND PRIEST.

[CHORUS.]

Lucky Omens blefs our Rites,
And fure Succefs fhall crown your Loves;
Peaceful Days and fruitful Nights,
Attend the Pair that fhe approves.

2

C A D M U S.

†Daughter, obey,
Hear, and obey.
With kind Confenting
Eafe a Parent's Care;
Invent no new Delay.

A T H A M A S.

†O hear a faithful Lover's Pray'r;
On this aufpicious Day
Invent no new Delay.

C A D M U S and *A T H A M A S.*

†Hear, and obey;
Invent no new Delay
On this aufpicious Day.

S E M E L E [*apart.*]

[RECITATIVE *accompany'd.*]

Ah me!
What Refuge now is left me?
How various, how tormenting,
Are my Miferies!
O *Jove* affift me.
Can *Semele* forgo thy Love,
And to a Mortal's Paffion yield?
Thy Vengeance will o'ertake
Such Perfidy.
       If I deny, my Father's Wrath I fear.

[SONG.]

O *Jove*, in Pity teach me which to chufe,
Incline me to comply, or help me to refufe.

† Omitted in 1925.

[SONG.]

The Morning Lark to mine accords his Note,
And tunes to my Diſtreſs his warbling Throat.
"Each ſetting, and each riſing Sun I mourn,
"Wailing alike his Abſence and Return.]

ATHAMAS.
[SONG. Ino.]

See, ſhe bluſhing turns her Eyes;
See, with Sighs her Boſom panting:
"If from Love thoſe Sighs ariſe,
"Nothing to my bliſs is wanting.

[SONG.]

Atha. *Hymen haſte, thy Torch prepare,*
Love already his has lighted;
One ſoft Sigh has cur'd Deſpair,
And more than my paſt Pains requited.

[Hymen, *haſte,* &c.]

INO.

Alas! ſhe yields,
And has undone me:
I can no longer hide my Paſſion;
It muſt have Vent ——
Or inward burning
Will conſume me.
O *Athamas* ——
I cannot utter it ——

ATHAMAS.

On me fair *Ino* calls
With mournful Accent,
Her Colour fading,
And her Eyes o'erflowing!

INO.

O *Semele!*

SEMELE.

On me fhe calls,
Yet feems to fhun me!
What wou'd my Sifter?
Speak ———

INO.

Thou haft undone me.

[A Four-Part Song.]

CADMUS.

Why doft thou thus untimely grieve,
And all our folemn Rites prophane?
Can he, or fhe, thy Woes relieve?
Or I? Of whom doft thou complain?

INO.

Of all; but all, I fear, in vain.

ATHAMAS.

Can I thy Woes relieve?

SEMELE.

Can I affwage thy Pain?

CADMUS, ATHAMAS and *SEMELE.*

Of whom doft thou complain?

INO.

Of all; but all, I fear, in vain

[It lightens, and Thunder is heard at a diſtance, then a Noiſe of Rain; the Fire is ſuddenly extinguiſh'd on the Altar: The Chief-Prieſt comes forward.

[Chorus *of* Prieſts.]

FIRST PRIEST.

Avert theſe Omens, all ye Pow'rs!
  Some God averſe our holy Rites controlls.
O'erwhelm'd with ſudden Night, the Day expires!
  Ill-boding Thunder on the Right Hand rolls
And *Jove* himſelf deſcends in Show'rs,
  To quench our late propitious Fires.

CHORUS of PRIESTS.

Avert theſe Omens, all ye Pow'rs!

[RECITATIVE *accompany'd.*]

SECOND PRIEST.

  "Again auſpicious Flaſhes riſe,
  "*Juno* accepts our Sacrifice.

[Flames are again kindled on the Altar, and the Statue nods.

THIRD PRIEST.

  "Again the ſickly Flame decaying dies:
  "*Juno* aſſents, but angry *Jove* denies.
              [The Fire is again extinguiſh'd.

ATHAMAS [apart.]

"Thy Aid, Pronubial *Juno, Athamas* implores.

SEMELE [apart.]

"Thee *Jove*, and thee alone, thy *Semele* adores.
      [A loud Clap of Thunder; the Altar ſinks.

[Chorus *of* Priests.]

FIRST PRIEST.

"Ceafe, ceafe your Vows, 'tis impious to proceed;
"Be gone, and fly this holy Place with Speed:
"This dreadful Conflict is of dire Prefage;
"Be gone, and fly from *Jove*'s impending Rage.

[*All but the Priefts come forward. The Scene clofes
on the Priefts, and fhews to View the Front and
Outfide of the Temple.* Cadmus *leads off* Semele,
Attendants follow. Athamas *and* Ino *remain.*

SCENE II.

ATHAMAS, INO.

ATHAMAS.

O *Athamas*, what Torture haft thou born!
And O, what haft thou yet to bear!
From Love, from Hope, from near Poffeffion torn,
And plung'd at once in deep Defpair.

INO.

[SONG.]

*Turn, hopelefs Lover, turn thy Eyes,
And fee a Maid bemoan,*
† *In flowing Tears and aking Sighs,
Thy Woes, too like her own.*

[*Turn, hopelefs Lover,* &c.]

† Omitted in 1925.

ATHAMAS.

She weeps!
The gentle Maid, in tender Pity,
Weeps to behold my Mifery!
So *Semele* wou'd melt
To fee another mourn.

Such unavailing Mercy is in Beauty found,
 Each Nymph bemoans the Smart
 Of every bleeding Heart,
But that where fhe her felf inflicts the Wound.

INO.

Ah me, too much afflicted!

ATHAMAS.

Can Pity for another's Pain
Caufe fuch Anxiety!

INO.

Cou'dft thou but guefs
What I endure;
Or cou'd I tell thee ——
Thou, *Athamas,*
Wou'dft for a while
Thy Sorrows ceafe, a little ceafe,
And liften for a while
To my Lamenting.

ATHAMAS.

Of Grief too fenfible
I know your tender Nature.
Well I remember,
When I oft have fu'd
To cold, difdainful *Semele*;
When I with Scorn have been rejected;

[SONG.]

Your tuneful Voice my Tale wou'd tell,
In Pity of my fad Defpair;
†"And, with fweet Melody, compel
"Attention from the flying Fair.

INO.

Too well I fee
Thou wilt not underftand me.
Whence cou'd proceed fuch Tendernefs?
Whence fuch Compaffion?
Infenfible! Ingrate! ——
Ah no, I cannot blame thee:
For by Effects unknown before,
Who cou'd the hidden Caufe explore?
Or think that Love cou'd act fo ftrange a Part,
To plead for Pity in a Rival's Heart.

ATHAMAS.

Ah me, what have I heard!
She does her Paffion own.

INO.

What, had I not defpair'd,
You never fhould have known.

†[DUET.]

You've undone me,
Look not on me;
Guilt upbraiding,
Shame invading;
Look not on me,
You've undone me.

† Omitted in 1925.

ATHAMAS.

With my Life I wou'd attone
Pains you've born, to me unknown.
Ceafe, ceafe to fhun me.

INO.

Look not on me,
You've undone me.

ATHAMAS.

Ceafe, ceafe to fhun me:
Love, Love alone
Has both undone.

INO, ATHAMAS.

Love, Love alone
Has both undone.

SCENE III.

"[To them] Enter CADMUS *attended.*

CADMUS.

" AH wretched Prince, doom'd to difaftrous Love!

" Ah me, of Parents moft forlorn!

"Prepare, O *Athamas*, to prove

"The fharpeft Pangs that e'er were born:

"Prepare with me our common Lofs to mourn.

3

ATHAMAS.

"Can Fate, or *Semele*, invent
"Another, yet another Punifhment?

[RECITATIVE *accompany'd.*]

CADMUS.

Wing'd with our Fears, and pious Hafte,
    From *Juno*'s Fane we fled;
Scarce we the brazen Gates had pafs'd,
When *Semele* around her Head
    With azure Flames was grac'd,
Whofe Lambent Glories in her Treffes play'd.
    While this we faw with dread Surprize,
    Swifter than Lightning downwards tending,
An Eagle ftoopt, of mighty Size,
    On Purple Wings defcending;
Like Gold his Beak, like Stars fhone forth his Eyes,
His Silver plumy Breaft with Snow contending:
    Sudden he fnatch'd the trembling Maid,
    And foaring from our Sight convey'd;
Diffufing ever as he leffening flew
Celeftial Odour, and Ambrofial Dew.

ATHAMAS.

†O Prodigy, to me of dire Portent!

INO.

†To me, I hope, of fortunate Event.

† Omitted in 1925.

SCENE IV.

Enter to them the Chief-Priest, with Augurs and
other Priests.

CADMUS.

SEE, fee, *Jove*'s Priests and holy Augurs come:
Speak, fpeak, of *Semele* and me declare the
Doom.

[Chorus of *Priests and Augurs*.]

FIRST AUGUR.

Hail Cadmus, *hail!* Jove *falutes the* Theban *King.*
    Ceafe your Mourning,
    Joys returning,
Songs of Mirth and Triumph fing.

SECOND AUGUR.

[SONG.]

    Endlefs Pleasure, endlefs Love
    Semele *enjoys above*;
    On her Bofom Jove *reclining,*
    Ufelefs now his Thunder lies,
    To her Arms his Bolts refigning,
    And his Lightning to her Eyes.

[CHORUS.]

    Endlefs Pleafure, endlefs Love
    Semele *enjoys above.*

FIRST PRIEST.

Hafte, hafte, hafte, to Sacrifice prepare,
Once to the Thunderer, once to the Fair:
 Jove *and* Semele *implore:*
Jove *and* Semele *like Honours fhare,*
  Whom Gods admire, let Men adore;
Hafte, hafte, hafte, to Sacrifice prepare.

Chorus of Priefts and Augurs.

Hail, Cadmus, *hail!* Jove *falutes the* Theban *King.*
  Ceafe your Mourning,
   Joys returning,
Songs of Mirth and Triumph Sing.

      [Exeunt omnes.

End of the Firft Act.

ACT II. SCENE I.

The SCENE *is a pleafant Country, the Profpect is*
terminated by a Beautiful Mountain adorn'd with
Woods and Water-falls. JUNO *and* IRIS *defcend in*
different Machines. JUNO *in a Chariot drawn by*
Peacocks; IRIS *on a Rainbow; they alight and meet.*

JUNO.

IRIS, impatient of thy Stay,
  From *Samos* have I wing'd my Way,
    To meet thy flow Return;

  Thou know'ft what Cares infeft
    My anxious Breaft,
And how with Rage and Jealoufie I burn:
    Then why this long Delay?

IRIS.

With all his Speed not yet the Sun
  Thro' half his Race has run,
Since I to execute thy dread Command
  Have thrice encompafs'd Seas and Land.

JUNO.

Say, where is *Semele*'s Abode?
    'Till that I know,
  Tho' thou hadft on Lightning rode,
  Still thou tedious art and flow.

IRIS.

[RECITATIVE *accompany'd*.]

Look where *Citheron* proudly ftands,
Bœotia parting from *Cecropian* Lands.
High on the Summit of that Hill,
Beyond the Reach of Mortal Eyes,
By *Jove*'s Command, and *Vulcan*'s Skill,
Behold a new-erected Palace rife.

[SONG.]

There from mortal Cares retiring,
She refides in fweet Retreat;
On her Pleasure, Jove *requiring,*
All the Loves and Graces wait.

[*There from,* &c.]

Thither Flora *the Fair*
With her Train muft repair,
Her amorous Zephyr *attending,*
All her Sweets fhe muft bring
To continue the Spring,
Which never muft there know an Ending.

Bright Aurora, *'tis faid,*
From her old Lovers Bed
No more the grey Orient adorning,
For the future muft rife
From fair Semele's *Eyes,*
And wait 'till fhe wakes for the Morning.

[Recitative *accompany'd.*]

J U N O.

No more——I'll hear no more.

How long muft I endure?——
How long with Indignation burning,
From impious Mortals
Bear this Infolence!

Awake *Saturnia* from thy Lethargy;
Seize, deftroy the curft Adultrefs.
Scale proud *Citheron*'s Top:
Snatch her, tear her in thy Fury,
And down, down to the Flood of *Acheron*
Let her fall, let her fall, fall, fall:

Rolling down the Depths of Night,
Never more to behold the Light.

If I am own'd above,
Sifter and Wife of *Jove*;
(Sifter at leaft I fure may claim,
Tho' Wife be a neglected Name,)

If I th'Imperial Scepter fway——I fwear
By Hell——
Tremble thou Univerfe this Oath to hear,
Not one of curft *Agenor*'s Race to fpare.

IRIS.

Hear mighty Queen, while I recount
What Obftacles you muft furmount;

[RECITATIVE *accompany'd.*]

With Adamant the Gates are barr'd,
    Whofe Entrance two fierce Dragons guard:
At each approach they lafh their forky Stings,
    And clap their brazen Wings:
    And as their fcaly Horrours rife,
        They all at once difclofe
        A thoufand fiery Eyes,
        Which never know Repofe.

JUNO.

[SONG.]

Hence, *Iris*, hence away,
    Far from the Realms of Day;
O'er *Scythian* Hills to the *Meotian* Lake
    A fpeedy Flight we'll take:
    There, *Somnus* I'll compell
His downy Bed to leave and filent Cell:

With Noife and Light I will his Peace moleſt,
Nor ſhall he ſink again to pleaſing Reſt,
'Till to my vow'd Revenge he grants Supplies,
And feals with Sleep the wakeful Dragons Eyes.

[*Hence*, Iris, &c.]

[*They aſcend.*

SCENE II.

The SCENE *changes to an Apartment in the Palace
of* Semele; *ſhe is ſleeping*; Loves *and* Zephyrs
waiting.

CUPID.

SEE, *after the Toils of an amorous Fight,*
　Where weary and pleas'd, ſtill panting ſhe lies;
While yet in her Mind ſhe repeats the Delight,
　How ſweet is the Slumber that ſteals on her Eyes!
　　Come Zephyrs, *come, while* Cupid *ſings,*
　　Fan her with your ſilky Wings;
　　　　New Deſire
　　　　I'll inſpire,
　　　And revive the dying Flames;
　　　　Dance around her
　　　　While I wound her,
　　　And with Pleaſure fill her Dreams.

A Dance of *Zephyrs,* after which *Semele* awakes,
and riſes,

SEMELE.

[SONG.]

O Sleep, why doſt thou leave me?
　Why thy viſionary Joys remove?
O Sleep, again deceive me,
　To my Arms reſtore my wandring Love.

SCENE III.

Two LOVES *lead in* JUPITER; *while he meets and embraces* SEMELE, CUPID *Sings.*

CUPID.

Sleep forsaking,
   Seize him waking;
Love has sought him,
Back has brought him;
Mighty Jove *tho' he be,*
And tho' Love cannot see,
   Yet by feeling about
   He has found him out,
   And has caught him.

SEMELE.

Let me not another Moment
Bear the Pangs of Abfence,
Since you have form'd my Soul for Loving,
No more afflict me
With Doubts and Fears, and cruel Jealoufie.

JUPITER.

[SONG.]

Lay your Doubts and Fears afide,
And for Joys alone provide;
Tho' this Human Form I wear,
Think not I Man's Falfhood bear.
   [*Lay your,* &c.]

You are Mortal, and require
Time to reſt and to reſpire.
   Nor was I abſent,

Tho' a while withdrawn,
To take Petitions
From the needy World.

While Love was with thee
I was preſent;
Love and I are one.

†[S O N G.]
S E M E L E.

If chearful Hopes
And chilling Fears,
Alternate Smiles,
Alternate Tears,
Eager Panting,
Fond Deſiring,
With Grief now fainting,
Now with Bliſs expiring;
If this be Love, not you alone,
But Love and I are one.

B O T H.

If this be Love, not you alone,
But Love and I are one.

[*Chorus of* Loves *and* Zephirs.
   How engaging, how endearing,
     Is a Lover's Pain and Care.]

  † The verses set by Handel were adapted from these
lines. In place of this song the recitative beginning "Now
all this Scene" and the song "Where'er you walk" (see
p. 30) were interpolated in 1925.

S E M E L E.

Ah me!

J U P I T E R.

Why Sighs my *Semele?*
"What gentle Sorrow
"Swells thy foft Bofom?
"Why tremble thofe fair Eyes
"With interrupted Light?
"Where hov'ring for a Vent,
"Amidft their humid Fires,
"Some new-form'd Wifh appears.
"Speak, and obtain.

S E M E L E.

At my own Happinefs
I figh and tremble;

Mortals whom Gods affect
Have narrow Limits fet to Life,
And cannot long be bleff'd.
Or if they could ——
A God may prove inconftant.

J U P I T E R.

Beware of Jealoufie:
Had *Juno* not been jealous,
I ne'er had left *Olympus,*
Nor wander'd in my Love.

S E M E L E.

With my Frailty don't upbraid me,
I am Woman as you made me.
Caufelefs doubting or defpairing,
Rafhly trufting, idly fearing.

If obtaining
Still complaining,
If confenting
Still repenting,
Moft complying
When denying,
And to be follow'd, only flying.
With my Frailty don't upbraid me,
I am Woman as you made me.

J U P I T E R.

Thy Sex of *Jove*'s the Mafterpiece,
Thou, of thy Sex, art moft excelling.
Frailty in thee is Ornament,
In thee Perfection.
Giv'n to agitate the Mind,
And keep awake Mens Paffions;
To banifh Indolence,
And dull Repofe,
The Foes of Tranfport
And of Pleafure.

S E M E L E.

Still I am mortal,
Still a Woman;
" And ever when you leave me,
"Tho' compafs'd round with Deities,
"Of Loves and Graces,
" A Fear invades me,
" And confcious of a Nature
"Far inferior,
"I feek for Solitude,
"And fhun Society.

J U P I T E R [*apart.*]

Too well I read her Meaning,
But muſt not underſtand her.
Aiming at Immortality
With dangerous Ambition,

She wou'd dethrone *Saturnia*;
And reigning in my Heart
Would reign in Heav'n.

[S O N G.]

Leaſt ſhe too much explain,
I muſt with Speed amuſe her;
It gives the Lover double Pain,
Who hears his Nymph complain,
And hearing muſt refuſe her.

[*I muſt,* &c.]

[*Chorus of* Loves *and* Zephirs.

Now Love that everlaſting Boy invites
To revel while you may in ſoft Delights.]

S E M E L E.

Why do you ceaſe to gaze upon me?
Why muſing turn away?
Some other Object
Seems more pleaſing.

J U P I T E R.

Thy needleſs Fears remove,
My faireſt, lateſt, only Love.

By my Command,
Now at this Inſtant,
Two winged *Zephyrs*
From her downy Bed

Thy much-lov'd *Ino* bear;
And both together
Waft her hither
Thro' the balmy Air.

SEMELE.

Shall I my Sifter fee!
The dear Companion
Of my tender Years.

JUPITER.

See fhe appears
But fees not me,
For I am vifible
Alone to thee.
While I retire, rife and meet her,
And with Welcomes greet her.
†Now all this Scene fhall to *Arcadia* turn,
The Seat of happy Nymphs and Swains,
There without the Rage of Jealoufie they burn,
And tafte the Sweets of Love without its Pains.

[SONG.]

Where'er you walk, cool Gales fhall fan the Glade;
Trees, where you fit, fhall croud into a Shade:
Where'er you tread, the blufhing Flow'rs fhall rife;
And all things flourifh where you turn your Eyes.

Where'er, &c.] [Exit.]

† See p. 26.

SCENE IV.

JUPITER *retires.* SEMELE *and* INO *meet and embrace. The* SCENE *is totally changed, and shews an open Country. Several Shepherds and Shepherdesses enter.* SEMELE *and* INO *having entertain'd each other in dumb Shew, sit and observe the Rural Sports, which end the Second Act.*

SEMELE.

Dear Sister, how was your Passage Hither?

INO.

O'er many States and peopled Towns we pass'd,
O'er Hills and Valleys, and o'er Desarts waste;
O'er barren Moors, and o'er unwholesome Fens,
And Woods, where Beasts inhabit dreadful Dens.
Thro' all which pathless Way our Speed was such,
We stop'd not once the Face of Earth to touch.
Mean time they told me, while thro' Air we fled,
That *Jove* did thus ordain.

ACCOMPANY'D.

But hark! the heav'nly Sphere turns round,
  And Silence now is drown'd
  In Ecstacy of Sound.
How on a sudden the still Air is charm'd.
As if all Harmony were just alarm'd!
And ev'ry Soul with Transport fill'd,
Alternately is thaw'd and chill'd.

DUET.

Prepare then, ye Immortal Choir,
Each sacred Minstrel tune his Lyre,
And all in Chorus join.

CHORUS.

Bless the glad Earth with heav'nly Lays,
And to that Pitch th'eternal Accents raise,
That all appear Divine.

ACT III.   SCENE I.

The SCENE is the Cave of Sleep. The God of Sleep
lying on his Bed. A soft Symphony is heard. Then
the Musick changes to a different Movement.

JUNO *and* IRIS.

JUNO.

S*omnus,* awake,
Raise thy reclining Head;

IRIS.

Thy self forsake,
And lift up thy heavy Lids of Lead.

[SONG.]

SOMNUS [waking.]

Leave me, loathsome Light;
Receive me, silent Night.
Lethe, *why does thy lingring Current cease?*
O murmur, murmur me again to Peace.

[Sinks down again.

IRIS.

Dull God, canst thou attend the Waters fall,
And not hear *Saturnia* call?

JUNO.

Peace *Iris*, Peace, I know how to charm him,
Pasithea's Name alone can warm him.

JUNO, IRIS.

Only Love on Sleep has Pow'r;
O'er Gods and Men
Tho' Somnus *reign,*
Love alternate has his Hour.

JUNO.

Somnus arise,
Disclose thy tender Eyes;
For *Pasithea*'s Sight
Endure the Light:
Somnus arise.

SOMNUS [rising.]

[SONG.]

More sweet is that Name
Than a soft purling Stream;
With Pleasure Repose I'll forsake,
If you'll grant me but her to sooth me awake.

[*More sweet*, &c.]

5

J U N O.

My Will obey,
She fhall be thine.
Thou with thy fofter Pow'rs
Firft *Jove* fhalt captivate,
To *Morpheus* then give Order,
Thy various Minifter,
That with a Dream in Shape of *Semele*,
But far more beautiful,
And more alluring,
He may invade the fleeping Deity;
†And more to agitate
His kindling Fire,
Still let the Phantom feem
To fly before him,
That he may wake impetuous,
Furious in Defire;
Unable to refufe whatever Boon
Her Coynefs fhall require.†

S O M N U S.

I tremble to comply.

J U N O.

To me thy leaden Rod refign,
To charm the Centinels
On Mount *Citheron*;
Then caft a Sleep on mortal *Ino:*
That I may feem her Form to wear,
When I to *Semele* appear.

[D U E T.]

Obey my Will, thy Rod refign,
And *Pafithea* fhall be thine.

† Omitted in the libretto but set by Handel.

SOMNUS.

All I muſt grant, for all is due
To *Paſithea,* Love and you.

JUNO.

Away let us haſte,
Let neither have reſt,
'Till the ſweeteſt of Pleaſures we prove;
'Till of Vengeance poſſeſs'd
I doubly am bleſs'd,
And thou art made happy in Love.

[*Ex* Juno *and* Iris.

[Somnus *retires within his Cave, the Scene changes*
to Semele's *Apartment.*

SCENE II.

SEMELE [*alone.*]

SEMELE.

I Love and am lov'd, yet more I deſire;
   Ah, how fooliſh a Thing is Fruition!
As one Paſſion cools, some other takes Fire,
And I'm ſtill in a longing Condition.
      Whate'er I poſſeſs
      Soon ſeems an Exceſs,
For ſomething untry'd I petition;
      Tho' daily I prove
      The Pleaſures of Love,
I die for the Joys of Ambition.

[SONG.]

My racking Thoughts by no kind Slumbers freed,
But painful Nights do joyful Days ſucceed.

SCENE III.

Enter JUNO *as* INO, *with a Mirrour in her Hand.*

JUNO [apart.]

THUS fhaped like *Ino*,
 With Eafe I fhall deceive her,
And in this Mirrour fhe fhall fee
Her felf as much transform'd as me.
Do I fome Goddefs fee!   [*To her.*
Or is it *Semele?*

SEMELE.

Dear Sifter fpeak,
Whence this Aftonifhment?

JUNO.

Your Charms improving
To Divine Perfection,
Shew you were late admitted
Amongft Celeftial Beauties.
Has *Jove* confented?
And are you made Immortal?

SEMELE.

Ah no, I ftill am Mortal,
Nor am I fenfible
Of any Change or new Perfection.

JUNO. [*Giving her the Glaſs.*

[RECITATIVE.]
Behold in this Mirrour
Whence comes my Surprize;
Such Luſtre and Terror
Unite in your Eyes,
†*That mine cannot fix on a Radiance ſo bright;*
Tis unſafe for the Senſe, and too ſlipp'ry for Sight.†

SEMELE. [*Looking in the Glaſs.*

O Ecſtacy of Happineſs!
Celeſtial Graces
I diſcover in each Feature!

[SONG.]
My ſelf I ſhall adore,
If I perſiſt in gazing;
No Objeƈt ſure before
Was ever half ſo pleaſing.
My ſelf, &c.

How did that Glance become me!
But take this flatt'ring Mirrour from me.
Yet once again let me view me.
Ah charming all o'er!
[*Offering the Glaſs, withdraws her Hand again.*
Here——hold, I'll have one Look more,
Tho' that Look I were ſure would undo me.

JUNO. [*Taking the Glaſs from her.*

Be wiſe as you are beautiful,
Nor loſe this Opportunity.
When *Jove* appears,
All ardent with Deſire,
Refuſe his proffer'd Flame
'Till you obtain a Boon without a Name.

† Omitted from the libretto but ſet by Handel.

SEMELE.

†Can that avail me?

JUNO.

Unknowing your Intent,
And eager for poſſeſſing,
He unawares will grant
The nameleſs Bleſſing.
But bind him by the Stygian *Lake,*
Leſt Lover-like his Word he break.

SEMELE.

But how ſhall I attain
To Immortality?

JUNO.

[Recitative *accompany'd.*]
Conjure him by his Oath
Not to approach your Bed
In Likeneſs of a Mortal,
But like himſelf, the mighty Thunderer,
In Pomp of Majeſty,
And heav'nly Attire;
†As when he proud *Saturnia* charms,
And with ineffable Delights
Fills her encircling Arms,
And pays the Nuptial Rites.†
By this Conjunction
With entire Divinity
You ſhall partake of heav'nly Eſſence,
And thenceforth leave this Mortal State
To reign above,
Ador'd by *Jove*,
In ſpite of jealous *Juno*'s Hate.

† Omitted from the libretto but set by Handel.

SEMELE.
[SONG.]

Thus let my Thanks be paid,
Thus let my Arms embrace thee;
And when I'm Goddeſs made,
With Charms like mine I'll grace thee.

JUNO.

Rich Odours fill the fragrant Air,
And *Jove*'s Approach declare.
I muſt retire ——

SEMELE.

Adieu——Your Counſel I'll purſue.

JUNO [*apart.*]

And ſure Deſtruction will enſue
Vain wretched Fool——[*To her.*] Adieu.
†[*Exit.*

SCENE IV.

JUPITER *enters, offers to embrace* SEMELE;
ſhe looks kindly on him, but retires a little from
him.

JUPITER.
[SONG.]

COme to my Arms, my lovely Fair,
 Sooth my uneaſie Care:
In my Dream late I woo'd thee,
And in vain I purſu'd thee,

† Here the song "*Above Measure*" (see p. 43) was interpolated in 1925.

For you fled from my Pray'r,
And bid me defpair.
Come to my Arms, my lovely Fair.

SEMELE.

Tho' 'tis eafie to pleafe ye,
And hard to deny;
Tho' Poffeffing's a Bleffing
For which I could die,
I dare not, I cannot comply.

JUPITER.

When I languifh with Anguifh,
And tenderly figh,
Can you leave me, deceive me,
And fcornfully fly?
Ah fear not. You muft not deny.

SEMELE, JUPITER.

I dare not, I cannot comply,
Ah fear not; you muft not deny.

JUPITER.

O *Semele,*
Why art thou thus infenfible?
Were I a Mortal,
Thy barbarous difdaining
Would furely end me,
And Death at my Complaining
In Pity would befriend me.

SEMELE.
[SONG.]

" *I ever am granting,*
  "*You always complain;*

"*I always am wanting,*
"*Yet never obtain.*

JUPITER.

Speak, fpeak your Defire,
I'm all over Fire.
Say what you require,
I'll grant it——now let us retire.

SEMELE.

Swear by the *Stygian* Lake.

JUPITER.

[RECITATIVE *accompany'd.*]
By that tremendous Flood I fwear,
Ye *Stygian* Waters hear,
And thou *Olympus* fhake,
In witnefs to the Oath I take.
                [*Thunder at a Diftance, and
                        underneath.*

SEMELE.

You'll grant what I require.

JUPITER.

I'll grant what you require.

SEMELE.

*Then caft off this human Shape which you wear,
And* Jove *fince you are, like* Jove *too appear;
    When next you defire I should charm ye.
        As when* Juno *you blefs,
        So you me muft carefs,
    And with all your Omnipotence arm ye.*

6

JUPITER.

[*Accompany'd.*]

Ah! take heed what you prefs,
For beyond all Redrefs,
Should I grant what you wifh, I fhall harm ye.

SEMELE.

† [SONG.]

I'll be pleas'd with no lefs,
Than my Wifh in Excefs;
Let the Oath you have taken allarm ye:
Hafte, hafte, and prepare,
For I'll know what you are;
So with all your Omnipotence arm ye.

SCENE V.

She withdraws, JUPITER *remains penfive and*
dejeded.

JUPITER.

[RECITATIVE *accompany'd.*]

AH! whither is fhe gone! unhappy Fair!
Why did fhe wifh?—Why did I rafhly fwear?
'Tis paft, 'tis paft Recall,
She muft a Victim fall.

Anon, when I appear
The mighty Thunderer,
Arm'd with inevitable Fire,

She needs muft inftantly expire.
'Tis paft, 'tis paft Recall,
She muft a Victim fall.

† This differs slightly from the version adopted by
Handel.

My softest Lightning yet I'll try,
And mildest melting Bolt apply:
In vain——for she was fram'd to prove
None but the lambent Flames of Love.
　　　'Tis past, 'tis past Recall,
　　　She must a Victim fall.

SCENE VI.

JUNO *appears in her Chariot ascending.*

JUNO.

† [SONG.]

ABove measure
Is the Pleasure
Which my Revenge supplies.
　　　Love's a Bubble
　　　Gain'd with Trouble,
And in possessing dies.
With what Joy shall I mount to my Heav'n again,
At once from my Rival and Jealousie freed!
The Sweets of Revenge make it worth while to reign,
And Heav'n will hereafter be Heav'n indeed.
　　　　　　　　　　　[She ascends.

[*Above measure,* &c.]

† See p. 39.

SCENE VII.

The SCENE *opening difcovers* Semele *lying under
a Canopy, leaning penfively. While a mournful
Symphony is playing fhe looks up and fees* Jupiter
*defcending in a black Cloud; the Motion of the
Cloud is flow. Flafhes of Lightning iffue from
either Side, and Thunder is heard grumbling in
the Air.*

S E M E L E.

[RECITATIVE *accompany'd.*]

AH me! too late I now repent
    My Pride and impious Vanity.
He comes! far off his Lightnings fcorch me.
—— I feel my Life confuming:
I burn, I burn—I faint—for Pity I implore—
O help, O help——I can no more.   [*Dies.*

As the Cloud which contains Jupiter *is arrived juft
over the Canopy of* Semele, *a fudden and great
Flafh of Lightning breaks forth, and a Clap of
loud Thunder is heard; when at one inftant*
Semele *with the Palace and the whole prefent
Scene difappears, and* Jupiter *re-afcends fwiftly.
The Scene totally changed reprefents a pleafant
Country, Mount* Citheron *clofing the Profpect.*

SCENE VIII.

Enter CADMUS, ATHAMAS *and* INO [*and Chorus of*
Priefts.]

INO.

†OF my ill-boding Dream
   Behold the dire Event.

CADMUS, ATHAMAS.   [ALL.]

O Terror and Aftonifhment.

[CHORUS.

Nature to each allots his proper Sphere,
But that forfaken, we like Meteors err:
Tofs'd thro' the Void, by fome rude fhock we're broke,
And all our boafted Fire is loft in Smoke.]

INO.

†How I was hence remov'd,
   Or hither how return'd, I know not:
   So long a Trance with-held me.
   But *Hermes* in a Vifion told me
       (As I have now related)
       The Fate of *Semele*;
   And added, as from me he fled,
   That *Jove* ordain'd I *Athamas* fhould wed.

CADMUS.

†Be *Jove* in ev'ry thing obey'd.
                         [*Joyns their Hands.*

† Omitted in 1925.

ATHAMAS.

†Unworthy of your Charms, my felf I yield;
Be *Jove*'s Commands and yours fullfill'd.†

‡ [SONG.

> *Defpair no more fhall wound me,*
> *Since you fo kind do prove.*
> *All Joy and Blifs furround me;*
> *My Soul is tun'd to Love.*]

CADMUS.

†See from above the bellying Clouds defcend,
And big with fome new Wonder this Way tend.

SCENE IX.

A bright Cloud defcends and refts on Mount
Citheron, *which opening difcovers* Apollo *feated*
in it as the God of Prophecy.

APOLLO.

[RECITATIVE *accompany'd.*]

APollo *comes to relieve your Care,*
And future Happinefs declare.

From Tyrannous Love all your Sorrows proceed,
From Tyrannous Love you fhall quickly be freed.

> *From* Semele's *Afhes a* Phænix *fhall rife,*
> *The Joy of this Earth, and Delight of the Skies:*
> *A God he fhall prove*
> *More mighty than Love,*

† Omitted in 1925.
‡ This Song was not printed in the libretto and was
omitted in 1925.

And a Sovereign Juice shall invent,
　　Which Antidote pure
　　The sick Lover shall cure,
And Sighing and Sorrow for ever prevent.

Then Mortals be merry, and scorn the blind Boy;
Your Hearts from his Arrows strong Wine shall defend:
Each Day and each Night you shall revel in Joy,
For when Bacchus *is born, Love's Reign's at an end.*

[CHORUS.]

Then Mortals be merry, &c.

Dance of Satyrs.

[CHORUS.

Happy, happy shall we be,
Free from Care, from Sorrow free;
Guiltless Pleasures we'll enjoy,
Virtuous Love will never cloy;
All that's Good and Just we'll prove,
And Bacchus *crown the Joys of Love.*]

[Exeunt omnes.

FINIS.

For EU product safety concerns, contact us at Calle de José Abascal, 56–1°,
28003 Madrid, Spain or eugpsr@cambridge.org.

www.ingramcontent.com/pod-product-compliance
Ingram Content Group UK Ltd.
Pitfield, Milton Keynes, MK11 3LW, UK
UKHW040616240426
470322UK00010B/144